LEARNING THROUGH
Noncompetitive
Activities and
Play

by Bill and Dolores Michaelis
with the editors of LEARNING Magazine

LEARNING Handbooks
530 University Avenue
Palo Alto, California 94301

Foreword

The imaginative movement projects in this handbook involve students in cooperation-building activities that enhance self-image and reinforce academic skills. Little preparation or equipment is necessary for these teacher-tested classroom alternatives to traditional physical competition.

The purpose of this and other LEARNING Handbooks is to help make teaching and learning more effective, interesting and exciting. Bill Michaelis is an Associate Professor of Recreation and Leisure Studies at California State Polytechnic University. Dolores Michaelis has taught at both the elementary and junior high school levels. Their extensive experience has been combined with Learning magazine's research facilities and editorial depth to produce this down-to-earth and lively handbook.

EDITOR: Carol B. Whiteley
DESIGNER: Catherine Flanders
ILLUSTRATIONS: Eileen Christelow
COVER: Photography by George B. Fry, III

EXECUTIVE EDITOR: Roberta Suid
EDITORIAL DIRECTOR: Morton Malkofsky
DESIGN DIRECTOR: Robert G. Bryant

Library of Congress Number: 77-89123
International Standard Book Number: 0—915092—12—3

Book Code: 016 • First Printing: August 1977

Dedication

To Julie, Fred, Helen, Ernie, Paige, Jason, Elaine, Gertrude

and all the rest

who helped keep the "kid" in us alive and well.

Contents

Introduction

This book is about using imaginative, largely noncompetitive physical activities as learning tools. Through these activities, children can learn to appreciate and develop their psychomotor, creative, affective, cognitive and social skills in an enjoyable, integrative way.

Every play book seems to have a research justification of the purpose of play; there's still a lot of belief in the primacy of the puritan ethic and the Listerine theory of education, that is, you've got to work hard and possibly endure hurt or a bad taste in your mouth in order to learn. But this book professes quite the opposite. It attempts to create smiles in an educational setting and strives to make learning a stimulating, motivating experience.

Here's how the activities in this book promote learning:

1. *The activities individualize the learning response.* There are many different solutions to the challenges in each activity. This

gives children the message that "I'm O.K. and important."

2. *The activities utilize the imagination and body orientation of children.* Research indicates that fantasy development is crucial to mental health and that there are strong connections between body image and self-concept.

3. *The activities encourage creativity.* Sutton-Smith, Hutt, Feitelson and Ross and others believe that creative play can be taught and that its benefits can be seen in measured improvement in general tests of creativity, flexible thinking, problem solving and other areas.

4. *The activities fully involve all the children.* Time is used efficiently and there is little standing in line or waiting around. There is greater development of skills per unit of time, affording greater opportunities for kids to be successful.

5. *The activities promote integrative learning.* We are total beings, not fractionated cognitive, affective or psychomotor entities. The more aspects of ourselves that we involve in the learning process, the greater its impact will be.

6. *The activities are largely nonregimented and noncompetitive.* Traditional body activities and physical education programs often give children the message that activity is something to be dreaded and that it must be highly structured. Physical activity is still often used as a punishment. And, with highly competitive activities, there are often more "losers" than "winners."

Our approach requires very few directions and little or no specialized equipment. We emphasize the joy of movement and ask the children to cooperate with their classmates in the solution of movement problems. Even in those activities that have competitive elements, the participatory ethic is emphasized, not winning or losing. This provides an effective, growth-filled counterbalance to the highly competitive nature of many traditional activities.

7. *The activities are fun as well as motivating.* Simply put, these activities say that play is O.K. They also say that learning can be joyful.

8. *The activities provide many peripheral benefits.* Increased social learning, the physiological benefits of gross motor activity, development of confidence in one's abilities, the benefits of laughter and relaxation and freedom of expression in both verbal and nonverbal ways are but a few of the additional benefits of noncompetitive physical play.

Chapter

1

The Teacher's Role—
You, Too, Can Fly!

here are two basic purposes to this chapter. The first is to acquaint you with the parameters of imaginative movement, an understanding that is crucial to everything in this handbook. Imaginative movement will be explained through the concepts of Finding Space/Knowing Space and Movement Through Space. The second purpose of the chapter is to provide you with suggestions and practical hints for getting started and for setting the proper classroom atmosphere.

The book is organized so that you begin with less threatening, less complex and more controlled forms of movement, and move on from there. In this sense the activities might be thought of as being age graded (beginning with primary activities at the start of each chapter or subheading and moving to intermediate activities). But don't feel you must do each chapter or activity in order. Do the activities at your own pace and in the sequence you feel most comfortable with. Each chapter may be used separately in whole or in part. The New Games activities may be played by all age groups.

Finding Space/Knowing Space

One of the most fundamental principles in imaginative movement teaching is that the child should have an awareness of his body in space; that is, he needs an understanding of his movement in relation to himself and in relation to others around him. To bring about this awareness he must be helped to distinguish between his "own" space and the "general" or "common" space of the area that he shares with others. During the initial imaginative movement activities you should reiterate these concepts regularly.

The following activities are three ways to teach and reinforce the concepts of "own" space and "general" space. All of them are good group warm-ups for later activities.

OBJECTIVE: To distinguish between one's "own" space and the "general" space in an area.

DESCRIPTION 1: NEAR—FAR

Make two hand-held signs in bold letters, one reading "NEAR" and the other "FAR." Hold up the "NEAR" sign and say, "Be as near to the wall as possible." Hold up the "FAR" sign and say, "Be as far from the wall as possible."

Try more directions, but start out with single simple commands, then try combinations, for example, "Be as near to the wall but as far from the ceiling as possible."

After several quick combinations, end up with this one: "Be as near to yourself but as far from everyone else as possible." This command will put the kids in their "own" space; tell them to sit down right where they are. Explain to them that the space they are in is their "own" space because they have enough room to reach out or spin around without touching anyone or anything except the floor. Tell them that in all the other movements in this activity they were using the "general" space.

DESCRIPTION 2: BUBBLES

Tell the children to look at all the space to play with in the room; this is the "general" space. Instruct them to stand so that each child has plenty of space around him. Say, "Imagine that you are inside a big bubble. Do you see where your bubble is located in the room? Your bubble is your very own space." Have the children touch the top, sides and bottom of their space. Have them try different movements inside their space, such as bending, stretching, jumping and so on.

Now, have the children move to the wall and come back to where they were without touching anyone or anything. You may want to tell them that their "bubble" will break if it touches anything. Remind them that they carry their "own" space with them wherever they move. Gradually increase their movement challenges (see "Moving Through Space" in this chapter and "Being Things" in Chapter 2) to promote understanding of "own" versus "general" space.

DESCRIPTION 3: MAGIC CIRCLE

Here's another approach to reinforcing the two concepts of space: Tell the children that a magic circle encloses each one of them. To understand the area of their circle, the kids should draw big circles in the air around their heads, around their middles, around their legs. Have them stretch as wide as they can in their circle, then scrunch as small as they can. Try having them spin around with their eyes closed or move around in different ways and on various levels (bottom, top, sides, middle) within their circle. Give them movement things to do as they take their circles with them around the "general" space.

Once the children understand the concept of space they are ready to explore the various ways of moving.

Moving Through Space

There are three main imaginative movement components. In actual practice they all interact with each other.

Imagination
This component involves both animate and inanimate things that move, real and imaginary things that move and the affective and environmental qualities of all of their movements. For example, you might ask the kids to show "how a kangaroo might hop when he's happy" or "how you would walk through gushy mud." (More will be said about imagination in "Being Things" in Chapter 2 and in other sections.) We believe that imagination is the primary motivator for physical movement activities.

Types of Movement
This category includes the two different ways in which we move: 1. Motor Fashion—in place (twisting, turning, pulling, stretching, bending) and 2. Locomotor Fashion—covering distance (running, walking, skipping, hopping [one foot to same foot], jumping [two feet to two feet], leaping [one foot to opposite foot], galloping, sliding, etc).

Movement Variables
These are the qualities of movement within which one combines imagination and motor or locomotor movement to design successful and fun movement challenges.
1. Space—In addition to "own" versus "general" space, this concept deals with various degrees of confinement (limited use of space) versus freedom (unlimited use).

2. Speed—This concept involves how fast or slow, at what rate of acceleration or deceleration one might move.

3. Levels—Crawling is at the lowest level; leaping through space would be one of the highest. In between are varying degrees of high, low and middle levels of movement (dissecting the vertical plane).

4. Direction—This includes forward, backward, in a straight line, sideways, zigzag, etc.

These are the variables we start with. As the children (and you) gain practice in using them with different types of imaginative movement, you can slowly begin adding variables such as these: **5.** Strength—light movements, powerful movements; **6.** Emotional Qualities—moving as if you were sad, happy, etc.; **7.** Utilizing Different Body Parts—"Can you move one part of you quickly while another is moved slowly?"; **8.** Relationships—self, partners or groups; **9.** Flow—smooth and sustained movement versus interrupted movement; **10.** Equipment—various ways of using balls, hoops, wands, beanbags, etc.

For more elaboration of the types and qualities of movement and for books of specific "challenges," see the Resource section of this book.

Teaching Imaginative Movement

To teach imaginative movement to your class you must first see the types of movement (running, pulling, etc.), the qualities of movement (speed, direction) and imagination as parts of a whole that work together. It may help you to make up cards listing possibilities from each of the three components. For example, you might write "run" on one card, "fast" on another and "the wind" on a third. Then you might give an imaginative movement challenge like this: "Can you run fast like the wind?" Other challenges might be: "Can you crawl slowly on your belly like a snake?" "Can you jump for joy all around the room?"

Your challenges may be very specific (like the above) or more general: "Move around the room as if you were mad." As you can see, the possibilities of combination are unlimited.

Here are a few general pointers:

1. The main ingredient in all of these activities is your enthusiasm. If you believe that these activities are important and exciting, you'll convey that excitement to your kids. Don't be afraid to participate in and enjoy all the games.

2. Though control is an important factor here, it shouldn't be an

overwhelming one. Set the structure yourself, but do have a definite start and stop signal. For example, "When I say GO, spin around like a top all over the room until you run out of energy, start to wobble and collapse gently onto the floor . . . GO." If you don't have a starting signal, one or two children will often start before you have completed the directions.

Many activities will stop themselves (all tops fall over); others you may have to stop yourself (some tops may never stop spinning). You will need a special word—perhaps "FREEZE." The children should learn that on the command they are to "freeze" in their tracks (no matter what they were doing). Their voices are frozen, also (however, their ears are not). GO-ing and FREEZE-ing (quick stops and starts) at the beginning of each activity period make an excellent "warm-up" for the children's minds, bodies and spatial awareness.

In addition to your forms of control, encourage the kids to use self-control. This does not mean rigidity, but it does mean avoiding crashing into or pushing others. Continue to emphasize the concept of one's "own" space even when one is moving in the "general" space. If things get out of hand you may wish to tell the children they are "electrodes," and if they crash they will short-circuit and must sit down a while.

3. Start with everyone seated in his own space (this will vary and each child does not have to be in the same space every time).

4. Ask for their attention while you give them their movement challenge.

5. It's best to start with less complex movements and increase to more complex. A less complex movement involves something in the child's imagination that he knows, and usually has only one movement: "Jump like a frog." As the children become familiar with basics, add more imaginative quality and movement components, such as, "What animals move with jumps?" "Are they different?" "Can you show us one and we'll try to guess what it is?" "How would you move if you were holding something big?" "Heavy?" "Suppose you were on ice with slippery shoes?" Or "How would you walk if you were tired and sleepy?" "Show us how you act when a loud balloon bursts right next to you." Ask the children for ideas.

Your challenges to the children can become more complex by adding more components, by requiring sequences of movements or by using more subtle interpretations. You can motivate older children with several additional "tricks" (see "Bigger Challenges" in Chapter 2).

6. Start slowly and gradually add speed. Emphasize "quality control" in the beginning stages. You want to avoid having your movement challenges dwindle to various interpretations of random running. To slow the kids down (other than with "FREEZE"), have them move at lower levels, backward or use hopping or jumping. You may even wish to use a tom-tom or tambourine to tell their feet how quickly or slowly to move. You could also try the activities in "slow motion."

7. In the beginning use confined, delineated spaces with individual responsibility and gradually move to greater degrees of spatial freedom and group relationships. Use a space that allows you to give verbal directions (when the group is "frozen") without having to raise your voice. Also, tell the children that they are responsible for their "own" space whether they are stationary or moving throughout the activity area. As individuals are capable of responding to a variety of movement challenges (given to the group as a whole) in a limited area, they are given more space, more freedom to explore. After each child has these basics down, it is best to come back to a limited area and begin partner work. The partner concept can prove to be a very useful organizing tool (see "Partner Activities" in Chapter 2).

8. Structure the activities loosely to encourage spontaneity and creativity, but make them directed enough to achieve the desired outcome. If the outcome is to be robots, consider whether or not to accept unrobotlike jumping beans. But if robots are to be made and a child is jumping up and down stiffly and mechanically, ask "What are you?" or "What kind of robot are you?" Try to be flexible.

9. Never take anything for granted, and always give the child the benefit of the doubt. Your directions may have been misunderstood or the child may have something else in mind that is perfectly acceptable. *Encourage individual, unique solutions.*

10. Remember that the ultimate goal of these activities is to develop freedom of expressiveness that is based on a broad range of experiences. Use only as much control as is necessary for you to develop confidence and for the children to focus on developmental challenges. Develop your own style, have fun and remember that you, too, can fly.

Chapter

2

Group Activities, Partner Activities

T he activities in this chapter are movement experiences designed for fun. They are grouped into three categories—Group Warm-Ups, Group Activities and Partner Activities—and can be done in a large room or on a playground. The warm-ups may be used before any of the activities in the book.

Group Warm-Ups

All of these are quickies (from 2 to 10 minutes). They are warm-up activities which require minimal words from you but which elicit maximal responses from the children.

A. BIG BLOW-UP

OBJECTIVE: To imitate an inanimate object using large muscles.
DESCRIPTION: Have the children find their own spaces. Then press together your thumb and two fingers as if you were holding a deflated balloon. Tell the children that you have a balloon in your hand and that each one of them is that balloon. Tell them, "I am going to blow you up." Pretend to blow up the "balloon." As you take a breath, say, "Can you feel yourselves getting filled with air? I'm going to blow you up bigger and bigger." Whenever you talk to the group, pinch the imaginary balloon so that "air" won't escape. Also

"freeze" the children in "balloon positions" until you stop talking and resume blowing. Keep blowing until you wish to stop (until the balloon is inflated) or blow until the balloon pops. At that point the kids will probably fall to the ground, but keep yourself open to other reactions. Take another "balloon" and try variations (see below).

MOTIVATIONAL HINTS/SPECIAL CONSIDERATIONS: To increase commitment to "being" a balloon, you might try asking each child what color or what kind of balloon (Mickey Mouse, long, round, etc.) he or she is. If a child does not wish to respond verbally, tell him that it is all right; you'll wait until he is blown up to discover what sort of balloon he is. Here are other ways to work with the "balloon":

VARIATIONS:

1. Blow up the balloon, then let the air out slowly (be prepared for some shrill sounds from the children).

2. Let go of the balloon (some children may fly around the room and then collapse, or some may just deflate where they are).

3. Blow up the balloon faster, slower; direct the size of the balloon yourself, for example, by holding a long balloon with two hands.

4. Have the balloon float in the air on a string.

5. Step on the balloon.

B. EGG BEATER

OBJECTIVE: To stretch the mind and body in preparation for later movement experiences.

DESCRIPTION: Have the children get in their own spaces. Hold up an imaginary (or real) egg beater and tell the children that they are all individual eggs that have been cracked into a giant mixing bowl. Say, "Feel how loose, wiggly and gooey you are." Tell the children that you are now going to scramble them, and they should show you with their bodies how they would move up and down and all around. Have them keep an eye on you, though, because sometimes you will beat them clockwise and sometimes you will beat them counterclockwise. If you stop the egg beater they should collapse smoothly and quietly onto the floor. But you might start it again. Keep up the element of suspense.

C. WASHING MACHINE

OBJECTIVE: To stretch the mind and body in preparation for later movement experiences.

DESCRIPTION: Ask the children to get in their own spaces. Tell them that the entire room is a giant washing machine and that each of them, except one child you choose to be the "agitator," is a piece of

clothing that will be washed in the machine. Tell them to select in their minds the piece of clothing they will be. Ask them, "What shape will it be?" "Will it be big or small?" "Will the fabric be silky smooth or heavy like blue jeans?" "What will it be like when it's moving and wet in the machine?" Have them show you by the way they move their bodies. Tell the "agitator" that his job is to stand in the middle of the room (the "washing machine") extending his arms and making twisting movements. Explain to him and the class how a washing machine cleans clothes if they do not already know, describing "wash," "rinse," "spin," etc.

Then say, "O.K., I'm ready to press the On button . . . there . . . can you feel yourself getting wet? . . . we're on the wash cycle now . . . rotate in and out and around the agitator . . . how do those soap bubbles feel?" You can then go to "rinse" and "spin" and add appropriate questions. You might even take all the "clothes" out of the "machine" after the last cycle, put them in a giant "dryer" and ask them to experience (through movement) how it feels to go from wet and crumply to warm and dry.

D. THREAD THE NEEDLE

OBJECTIVE: To promote stretching, individual challenges, body flexibility and balance.

DESCRIPTION: Ask each child to get in his own space facing you. Then ask the group if they have ever seen anyone thread a needle. Remind them that to do this you have to be very steady. Tell them that their arms will be a needle hole and their legs will be the thread. Have each child hold his arms in front of himself and touch his fingertips together while he bends slightly forward at the waist. Then have them try to step through the "hole," one foot at a time, without having their fingertips lose contact with each other. Be prepared for a couple of groans, a few giggles and a couple of people falling over. If they've gotten both feet through, have them step back through (again, one foot at a time) so that they will be in their original positions.

VARIATIONS: Here are a few similar activities:

1. Instead of just touching fingertips, have the children clasp their hands together (interlocking fingers) and try it.

2. Have them try it without touching their hands at all.

3. If some kids have difficulty with all of the possibilities, have them practice by holding a wand (stick) horizontally in front of them, grasping it with both hands and stepping through (over the wand). Start with longer wands and gradually use shorter ones as the

children gain more balance and flexibility.

E. COFFEE GRINDER (or Blender)
OBJECTIVE: To promote arm strength, body support, alignment and coordination.
DESCRIPTION: Ask the children to get in their own spaces facing you. Then say, "Have you ever seen how the blades inside a grinder or blender go around and around to chop and mix everything up?" (Explain the action to them if they are unfamiliar with these appliances.) "We're going to pretend that each one of us is one of those blades." Have the children stand, put one hand down on the floor and straighten their bodies so that they are in a side-leaning position with the bulk of their weight being supported by the extended arm. Each child then walks or scoots around the hand of the extended arm, making a circle. They should try to go slowly at first and keep their bodies fairly rigid.
VARIATIONS: After a few times around, have the kids switch arms and move in the opposite direction; try going backward as well as forward; give them some quick-change commands: "left (left arm extended, body moving around to the left) . . . right . . . backward . . . forward," and so on.

F. AUNT DINAH'S DEAD (or Queen Didoe's Dead)
OBJECTIVE: To provide a physical warm-up and opportunities to use imagination, leadership and mimicking.
DESCRIPTION: This is an old folk game that is really a jazzed-up version of "Follow the Leader." Its main distinction lies in the mention of the tabooed areas of death and dying.

Have the children stand or sit in a circle. Then you walk around in the center of the circle and say, "Aunt Dinah's dead."

The children should ask, "How'd she die?"

You reply, "A doin' this," while you hop, jump, pantomime, make funny faces or the like.

Then the children should say, "A doin' this?" while they do the same action you have just done.

You may repeat "Aunt Dinah's Dead" as many times as you like, doing different stunts. Then, when you'd like someone else to be the leader, say, "Aunt Dinah's livin'."

The children should respond, "Where's she livin'?"

Then you and the children together say, "She's livin' in the country, she's movin' to town: she's a shruggin' her shoulders and a truckin' on down."

27

You then call a child's name to take your place in the center of the circle. That child may pick his or her successor, and so on.

VARIATIONS: Although a great deal of the appeal of this game is in the folk rhyme, a quicker version can be played with a group randomly spread out in their own spaces. (They may even stand in line.)

First, say to the class as you stand in front of them, "Aunt Dinah's dead."

The children should say, "How'd she die?"

You say, "She died like this," and do a motion. Everyone should mimic that motion. You can do a designated number of actions and then pick the next leader. (Each child can then pick a leader to follow him.) Encourage each child to be a good leader and follower and to think of new, funny or challenging actions.

G. IMAGINARY ROPES

OBJECTIVE: To provide a quick warm-up for the imagination and the body—particularly jumping and balancing abilities.

DESCRIPTION: Ask the children to get in their own spaces and face you (or the designated leader). Hold in front of you an imaginary jump rope. You can indicate by your movements that it is an individual jump rope big enough for you. Indicate to the children that each of them also has a rope that is just the right size for them. Say, "Are you holding it by the ends? Now let's see, what are some things we can do with our ropes?" Some imaginary possibilities are:

1. Jump forward (the rope goes over the head from back to front—the "usual" way).

2. Jump backward (the rope goes from front to back).

3. Gallop around the room while jumping rope.

4. Fold the rope in half and hold it by the ends in one hand. Try circular rope skipping by swinging the rope under the feet in circular fashion, jumping it each time.

5. Do balancing activities—walking forward and backward on the rope, being careful not to fall in Alligator River.

6. Have a tug of war between the left arm and the right arm, the left leg and the right arm, etc.

H. WHO STARTED THE MOTION? (or Indian Chief)

OBJECTIVE: To promote leadership, the ability to follow and the ability to distinguish quick changes.

DESCRIPTION: This game has a degree of competition in that the "It" is trying to guess who the leader is; the main interactions it promotes, however, are leadership and cooperation. This activity reenforces the important lesson that each child needs to be both a good leader and a good follower.

Have the children sit in a circle, either in chairs or on the floor. Choose one child to be "It" and have him turn his back to the group and hide his eyes. Then point to one child who will be the leader. Ask the leader to stay in his place and start any continuous action with his hands, fingers, feet, etc. For example, he could tap the floor with his hands. Everyone else in the circle must follow the leader's actions. The leader may change his movements any time he feels it is safe (when he thinks the "It" isn't looking). Once the motion has started, have the "It" open his eyes and stand in the center of the circle. Tell him he has three guesses to find out who the leader is. You can also try this game with everyone standing in a circle.

MOTIVATIONAL HINTS/SPECIAL CONSIDERATIONS: With a clever leader and quick followers, the "It" will have difficulty guessing correctly. If this is the case time after time, try these hints to increase the success of the "It."

1. Tell him "It's someone with blue on . . . (etc.)"

2. You can have the "It" stand on the perimeter of the circle (rather than in the center). This affords him a view of the entire circle and increases the probability of his catching the leader.

3. Tell the leader when to change the motion.

Group Activities

A. BEING THINGS

OBJECTIVE: To provide continued imaginative practice in selected motor movements.

DESCRIPTION: Have you ever thought of all the things around us which move that could be utilized for imaginative/developmental purposes? Children have, and in their dramatic free play we see broomsticks become motorcycles and arms become wings that fly them above the buildings. Here are a few of the many categories of things that move or express movement and a few of the items in those categories: a. Animals—horses, kangaroos, swans; b. People—cowboys, jackhammer operators, dancers; c. Machines —motorcycles, screwdrivers, drills, washers; d. Play Objects—balls, seesaws, toys; e. Objects in Nature—wind, leaves, snow, water; f. Appliances and Kitchen Objects—vacuum cleaners, egg beaters, toasters; g. Everyday Miscellany—firecrackers, popcorn, rubber bands; h. Theme Movements—circus, farm, rodeo; i. Make-Believe—

giants, superman, bionic woman, monsters; j. Emotions and Other Qualities—sad, tired, warm; k. Contrasts—hot vs. cold, fast vs. slow.

Using these objects and others you may think of, have your class try to "be" things that move. Ask them to find their own spaces and then ask questions like these: "Can you move like . . . ?" "How would you move if . . . ?" "Who can move like . . . ?" As with the other movement challenges, start simply and add more complexity and subtlety as you go on.

Another way of approaching "Being Things" might be for you to first list all the movement types and qualities and then list the imaginative possibilities under each category. For example:

TYPES

ROLLING	JUMPING	TWISTING	SLIDING
balls	frogs	screwdriver	baseball player
logs	kangaroos	"The Twist"	on ice
rocks	rabbits	traffic cop	slip and slide
wheels	pogo sticks	cyclone	shuffleboard pieces

QUALITIES

SPEED	LEVELS	DIRECTIONS
tortoises	giants	merry-go-rounds
cheetahs	elves	wind mills
motorcycles	toasters	down the up escalator
car running out of gas	jack-in-the-box	basketball players

It's easy to see from these approaches that the whole range of motor and locomotor responses could be built into an imaginative physical activity curriculum.

B. WHO CAN? CAN YOU?

OBJECTIVE: To develop complex motor skills through creative challenges.

DESCRIPTION: What follows are some samples of "Who Can?" statements that involve creative individual solutions to movement problems. They can be taught as individual or group challenges.

Bending

Who can make a shape by bending four parts of their body?
Who can lie down and bend as many parts of their body as possible?

Is it easier to lie on your stomach, your back or your side when you do this?

Stretching

Can you stretch your whole body as slowly as possible? Who can stretch just one part very slowly? Another part?

Pulling

Who can find a partner and take turns discovering ways to pull each other up from the floor?

Who can pull their partner using different parts of their body (knees, fingers, etc.)?

Pushing

Who can pretend to push a refrigerator? Is it easier to push it from a higher or lower level? Can you feel it?

Can you discover different ways to push and then pull your partner? Which are the best ways?

Turning

Who can make two parts of their body turn? How many parts can you turn at the same time? In different directions?

Twisting

Who can twist their body slowly from side to side?

How do your arms help you twist?

Can you twist some of your body parts around other parts?

Lifting

Who can work with two helpers and discover ways to lift each other off the floor?

Swinging

Who can swing two body parts in the same direction?

Who can swing two parts in opposite directions?

Rocking

Who can rock their body in many different ways?

Walking

Who can pretend that they are hiking up a steep mountain? Do you walk in a different way? Why?

Can you walk with your knees way up in the air?

Have you ever seen anyone walk this way? Who?

Running

Who can run with their hands in different places? At their sides? With their arms out to their sides or over their head? What are some times that you would run in these ways? Which positions are easiest? Hardest?

Leaping

Can you leap over one partner? Over two partners?

Jumping
Who can jump and keep their legs moving while in the air?
Who can put a ball between their knees and jump all around the
room without losing the ball?
Hopping
Who can bend their body in different ways while they are hopping?
Skipping
Can you skip fast using long skips? Using short skips? Which is
easier?
Sliding
Who can slide around the room while balancing a beanbag on their
head?

C. SPORTS MOVEMENTS

Up to this point we have dealt with beginning-level warm-ups and
challenges; what follows is a series of activities utilizing the complexity of elaborated movement and expressiveness.

OBJECTIVE: To explore and practice the complexity of sports-
related movements.

DESCRIPTION: Before you begin to explore sports movements, iso-
late the component movements of the sport(s) you will be working
with. This is really easy even if you're not a sports nut and have only
occasionally seen a sports event.

First, ask yourself this question: What ways do people move in
(e.g.) baseball? (They throw, hit, bend, stretch, run, catch, at the
simplest level of analysis.) Then ask, in what *ways* do they hit, run,
etc.? (They bend at the knees and hold the bat high, etc.) If you're not
sure, ask the kids; they'll tell you.

Once you have done this for your sport, you are ready for some
activities. You can make them as simple or complex as you like. You
can also use several sports to practice similar movements. For example, "What are some different sports in which we jump?" (dancing,
basketball, skating, skiing, etc.) "How are those jumps similar . . .
different?" Here are more specifics:

1. Have everyone in his or her own space. Ask the children how a
person looks when he or she is taking a jump shot in basketball.
Pretend you are a teammate. Quickly pass the "ball" to the group.
They are to make a jump shot. Do a series of quick passes and shots.
Are the kids jumping as high as they can and releasing the ball at the
top of their jump? Have the children become guards in a basketball
game, guarding a player who is making a jump shot. How would
they move then? ("Does thrusting your arms up in the air as you

jump help you go higher?") Have the kids play around with the possibilities of a sports scenario. They can be dribbling in and out of "each other," moving around the room bouncing the "balls" high, low, fast, slow, etc.

2. Utilize a wide variety of sports and movements. Start the kids in their own spaces (stationary) first and then let them explore the movements in the general space. Ask them to show you how it looks to make a football kick, to swim the backstroke, to hit a forehand or backhand, etc. Have them maintain a clear focus and exhibition of the movements that you suggest.

D. IMAGINARY TUG OF WAR

OBJECTIVE: To experience without using equipment an activity that generally uses equipment.

DESCRIPTION: Preface this activity with a discussion of what happens when you are having a tug of war. Ask the kids questions like these: Do the people nearest the middle of the rope need to pull the most, or do those on the ends? How does your body move when you pull the rope? Do you ever let go of the rope? What happens when one side seems to be pulling harder than the other? The other side moves closer to the center line, right? There's a give and take—both sides cannot be moving back at the same time . . . .

After the discussion, start the tug of war. (Again, the purpose of this activity is not to win the tug of war but to concentrate on the actions and reactions, the give and take of the activity.) Divide the children evenly into two "teams" and tell them they are holding a rope. Have the children in each team stand in a row and give each child part of the "rope" to hold—all the while showing with your own movements how heavy it is, remarking how rough and fuzzy it is, and so on. Then say "GO" and have both sides tug. As they pull, say, "Feel the rope in your hands, hold on tight—stay behind the person in front of you. Watch the other team and react—if they move back, you have to move forward. Feel your body stretching, straining against the pull of the rope . . . feel it down to your toes . . . ."

MOTIVATIONAL HINTS/SPECIAL CONSIDERATIONS: If it's hard for the kids to concentrate or really "feel" the "rope," you can take them on an imaginary journey looking for hemp in the forest to make the rope with; you can also take an imaginary trip to the store to purchase some rope. How long is it? How thick will it need to be? How heavy is it? Create the commitment to experiencing the activity in this way. Then try it again (see "Variations" below) or try it on another day.

VARIATIONS: You may want to try this activity before the group tug of war. First, ask the children to get in the own spaces. Then, tell them that they are a rope. You will be telling them which way to be pulled: "I'm pulling your right arm . . . now your right leg . . . left arm . . . right arm . . . you are tight and stretched . . . I'm pulling your head straight up . . . now I'm pulling your right arm and left arm away from each other . . . oops! your right arm is moving further away . . . what's your left arm doing?" (It should be more slack—bodies should be pulling to the right.)

After this activity the children should be more aware of how groups move a rope during a tug of war.

E. MOVING TO COLORS AND SOUNDS

OBJECTIVE: To provide practice in reacting to auditory stimuli; to encourage large-muscle coordination and creative expression.

DESCRIPTION: Ask each child to find his or her own space. Explain that you will call out a color and that each color will be the signal for a specific movement. For example, if you say "red," the children should hop; "blue," skip; "green," crawl; "yellow," spin around (use as many colors as ability level will permit).

MOTIVATIONAL HINTS/SPECIAL CONSIDERATIONS: Say the colors slowly at first to give the children time to remember the movement for each. Coach those who don't remember as quickly as others. Start out with two or three colors and add more when the first ones are memorized. Make certain that the kids know not to bump into each other.

For young children you might like to use pieces of different-colored construction paper, combining visual with auditory stimuli by holding up the red piece of paper when you say "red," etc. You could also hold up the paper but not say the corresponding color word.

VARIATIONS: There are a number of possible variations:

1. For older players, give each color two or three directions, e.g., red = hop on right foot, touch floor, hop on left foot.

2. Try using numbers instead of colors, for example, 1 = skip to wall; 2 = do a somersault, etc.

3. Use sounds instead of colors, for example, a verbal beep-beep = hop; a tongue clack = touch toes, etc. A prepared list of sounds and corresponding movements might be useful.

4. After you feel comfortable with the original activity you may wish to try a less structured, more imaginative one. Make continuous sounds (lots of beeps, for example), instructing the children to

move in the general space however the sound makes them want to move. Whichever way the child wants to move is acceptable, as long as she covers ground. (For an "initial structure" tool you can start the children in a circle, have them all move in their own way to the right, then to the left.) Then ask the children to find their own spaces and move in them to another sound, perhaps a series of high-pitched beeps. They might react by tiptoeing with tiny steps. If you switch to booming beeps, movement may become more pronounced—trudging or stomping. Other sounds you can try are tongue-trilling, whirrs, clangs, booms and siren wails. Vary their pitch, intensity, volume and rhythm.

This variation expands creative expression and can release inhibitions. Encourage your kids to make full use of the space above, below and to each side of their bodies—they can stretch high, crouch low, spread wide and so on.

F. BIGGER CHALLENGES

OBJECTIVE: To develop increased sophistication of movement through more complex challenges and gamelike activities.

DESCRIPTION: As the children master the basics of imaginative movement, they may need more sophisticated problem solving in order to maintain motivation. To do this you can provide more difficult challenges that ask the kids to do one or more of the following (or any others that you make up):

1. Jump and stretch as high as possible; then curl and roll on the floor. Repeat several times.

2. Get into a position where at least one leg is higher than the rest of your body. Change to another position but be sure that at least one leg is higher than every other part.

3. Combine a series of runs and skips to move about in any direction except forward.

4. See how many ways you can move forward without standing upright.

5. Perform some running and turning movements with a partner.

6. How many ways can you spin using different parts of your body?

7. Keep one foot stationary on the floor. How many ways can you stretch the rest of your body? How far away from your foot can you reach?

You can also make challenges more difficult by suggesting that each child develop routines of movement similar to a gymnastic exhibition. These can be written out on a card and practiced. A variation of this would be to assign a group challenge or routine. The cards could then be shuffled and exchanged to provide a variety of interpretative responses to the same problem. Here are two examples:

a. Perform a movement sequence that includes the following (not necessarily in this order): four walks, two hops, a running movement. Within your sequence there should be two changes of direction, a strong angry movement and a change of pace.

b. With three other people, develop a routine that takes about two minutes and includes these movements: movements at two different levels; light, smooth, accelerating movements; side-by-side backward movements; leaps and jumps; movements that use most of the general space; lifting and balancing; spinning movements; movements that express joy or happiness.

Another way for older kids to practice movement variables is through the use of a series of tasks. Again, preparation for this is minimal and results in a lot of challenge and activity. Directions can be typed on cards and varied weekly; simple stations can be set up to move among. Here's an example (stations are numbered):

1	3	5	7
leap to 2	jump rope to 4	do something silly to 6	do something upside down to 8

4	6	8	2
balance beanbag on head; walk backward to 5	move 2 body parts; vary speed to 7	hop sideways to 1	spin at low level to 3

Partner Activities
Partner activities can be a good organizing tool. The activities in this section progress from simple to more complex.

A. WRING THE DISHRAG
OBJECTIVE: To develop partner cooperation and upper-body (arm and shoulder) flexibility.
DESCRIPTION: Have the kids get in their own spaces. Ask them if they have ever seen anyone wring out a sponge, washcloth or dishrag; have them discuss the motion. Then have them find a partner and sit down next to him or her. Say, "The two partners are going to be a giant dishrag and are going to work together to wring out all of their water. This is how it is done." Demonstrate the twisting motion

with a child or have two children "wring themselves out." Do this by asking two kids to face each other and join hands. Have them raise and join one pair of arms (left for one and right for the other) and rotate (turn) under that pair of arms, without letting go of their hands. Tell them to continue around until they are back to their original position.

SPECIAL CONSIDERATIONS: If some kids turn too quickly or have trouble making a complete circle, tell them to go slowly at first. Remind them to be careful and not bang into their partner.

VARIATIONS: Once they have been successful at one or two slow circle turns, the kids may pick up speed a bit and do a series of turns, first in one direction and then in the other.

B. GET UP AND BOOGIE/GET DOWN TO BUSINESS

OBJECTIVE: To learn cooperation, coordination and trust; in larger groups it is excellent for building group unity.

DESCRIPTION: This activity is a good organizing tool with many variations. To begin, have two children sit back to back on the floor. Have them lock their arms together and keep their backs flat against each other. Tell them to bend their knees and keep their feet as flat on the floor as possible. From this position both children should try to stand by pushing against each other's back (they shouldn't move their feet).

MOTIVATIONAL HINTS: Some children will be able to do the activity right away while others will have more difficulty. The tricks to standing easily are communicating with each other and applying even pressure and movement. Initially, allow the kids to explore what works and what doesn't. You may want to have a successful pair demonstrate for the rest of the group. Also, although it's not crucial, you may wish to pair children who are approximately the same size. Try to do this activity in gym shoes or on a nonskid surface.

VARIATIONS: Once the majority of the group is able to do the exercise, have them change partners and see if they can do it with others, i.e., boy-girl, tall-short, etc. It may be helpful for a successful pair to verbalize how they do it. Some kids may get frustrated but give them motivation and allow them plenty of time. Some other variations are as follows:

1. Once the partners have learned to get up, see if they can go back down very slowly to a sitting position (not just flop down).

2. Once they have mastered this degree of control, have them attempt to walk like a spider (arms still locked, back to back) from the

halfway-down position.

3. Have the partners try to stand up or sit down with their arms at their sides, just using back pressure to accomplish their goal.

4. Have the partners experiment with controlled-movement cooperation in an exercise called "Elevators." Have them stand back to back, keeping their hips and shoulders touching and their arms at their sides. Tell them to keep pressing as they inch their feet forward and take their "elevator" down together. How far down can they take it without falling? Have them keep pressing and slowly bring their elevator back up again. When they've got these motions mastered, have them try raising and lowering their "elevator" several times on their own.

5. This exercise can be tried with three or more people in a group—the more people, the more difficult the movements will be because greater levels of cooperation and communication are required. You can start with threes, and work your way up. Begin with each group sitting on the floor, locking arms, with backs and hips as tightly pressed together as possible.

C. BUSY BEES

OBJECTIVE: To encourage being physically close in a nonthreatening manner; to encourage cooperation with a partner in following directions; to learn body parts.

DESCRIPTION: Ask the children to find a partner and get in their own spaces. Call out a body part in this manner: "head-to-head." Tell each partner to touch his head (or the part you called) to that of his partner *in any way* both choose, and then go back to their original positions. Follow with another part—"knuckle-to-knuckle"—and another—"shin-to-shin." You may have to point to a part on your own body if, after having called it out, the children do not know where the part is on their own bodies. Don't show the children how to connect with their partners; what ever way they choose to do this is acceptable, as long as both partners use the body part you have designated.

Tell the group that the magic words "Busy Bees" are the signal for them to find a new partner—one they haven't had before. (Later you may wish to ask the group for other words to use as the signal.) After you have called out several parts, say "Busy Bees!" Wait until all the kids have new partners (after playing for a while you may wish to check that each child is choosing a new partner each time). Continue the game until you decide to stop or until all combinations of partners have been exhausted.

MOTIVATIONAL HINTS/SPECIAL CONSIDERATIONS: Your enthusiastic attitude and the element of surprise—"Busy Bees"—can keep this activity going indefinitely. The first time you try it, however, you may wish to make up a list of body parts ahead of time; you can repeat parts because it is likely there will be new partners. If appropriate, try using more "out of the way" body parts such as the back of the knee, the waist, the instep and so on. Unless you designate that plural parts are to be used (e.g., both knees rather than one knee), accept from the children whatever choice they choose.

Sometimes children may get embarrassed if they have an opposite-sex partner. If this happens, don't force the issue. Let them sit out the activity, if they wish, until you call "Busy Bees" and there is a partner change. If they decide to play, limit the body parts to those that are least threatening.

VARIATIONS: There are a number of ways to vary this activity:

1. For older kids you might use technical terms, for example, "femur-to-femur," "scapula-to-scapula," "ulna-to-ulna."

2. For learning left and right and for understanding the mirror concept (when a person is facing you, his left is on your right), try "right thumb-to-right thumb," "left shoulder-to-left shoulder" and the like.

3. You can turn the fun into a game called "Twister." Have the children keep the first-call body parts connected when the second call is given, for example, when "ankle-to-ankle" is followed by "knees-to-knees," ankles and knees stay connected. You then can add "shoulders-to-shoulders." A topple will probably ensue, but the game should be a great source of fun and laughter.

D. BRIDGES, WALLS, LOGS, BALLS, TOPS, HOPS

OBJECTIVE: To encourage large-muscle activity, creative individuality, cooperation and expressiveness.

DESCRIPTION: Have the children choose a partner. One of each set of partners becomes a bridge (in this activity, a bridge is something that you crawl under); the other becomes the "crawler." The only requirement for being a bridge is that someone must be able to crawl under it. The bridges may stand with their legs apart, may lie on their back or belly up, may be sideways, on all fours, whatever.

At your signal, have the bridges (half the group) get into position. When you say "GO," the "crawlers" must crawl as quickly as possible under as many bridges as they can. Let the action continue without interruption for about 15 to 20 seconds. Then call out "CHANGE." The bridges then become crawlers and the crawlers bridges. Wait another short interval and call out "CHANGE" again. You can call "CHANGE" quickly and at funny times, for example, when a crawler is directly under a bridge. You can also call "FREEZE"—all action is to stop; "REDIRECT"—crawlers are to change the direction in which they are going; and "RELAX"— everyone can get out of their position and rest. Think of different ways the crawlers might move, for example, feet first.

MOTIVATIONAL HINTS/SPECIAL CONSIDERATIONS: You may want to have the children remove hard-soled shoes so they won't hurt other children.

Doing the activity in partners can be an initial organizing tool; after a few minutes, let the kids move in the general space and interact with the whole group. Continue the rule that half the kids should be in one "role," the other half in the other "role."

VARIATIONS: Here are a few variations:

1. Walls. Have the children find a partner. One is the wall, the other the jumper. Say, "Jump, leap or vault over as many walls as you can."

2. Logs. In this game each partner is either a log or a log roller. A log is someone lying still on the ground with his arms over his head. A log roller is one who rolls a log by pushing (rolling) it around with his hands, attempting to avoid a log jam, although it appears that sometimes the fun is in creating a jam. This activity is good for promoting closeness and touch in a nonthreatening way.

3. Balls. One partner is a ball—he keeps his knees loose and bouncy. The other partner is the ball bouncer who stands next to her "ball" and places her hand lightly (yet firmly for "control") on the ball's head. At "GO," the bouncer bounces the ball (the "ball" should move up and down as he walks in response to the bouncer's hand movement) while you say, "Bounce the ball this high . . . When I say CHANGE, all bouncers become balls, all balls become bouncers . . . can you bounce using two hands?"

4. Tops. Have each child find a partner. One partner is a top, the other the top spinner. The top's arm is the string that is wound around the top in order to make it spin. The top spinner pulls the "string" and the top spins around the general space until it runs out of energy, teeters and finally falls to the ground, waiting to be spun again. As they spin, say, "Can you spin the top the other way this time? CHANGE."

5. Hops. Ask the partners to face each other. Have one partner extend his right (or left) leg and have the other partner grab his ankle. At the same time have the second partner extend the same leg and let

the first partner grab his ankle. Make sure that both partners are holding right (or left) ankles. Tell them to hop around the room together. Have them change legs or partners when they get tired.

E. BIG AND LITTLE INGS

OBJECTIVE: To practice using large muscles for big and little movements.

DESCRIPTION: Prepare a list of words ending in -ing. You may use purely physical words, such as hopping, skipping and crawling, and quality words, such as horrifying, pleasing, loving. Then play the game, using this as a guide:

Big	Little
B_1	L_1
B_2	L_2
B_3	L_3
B_4	L_4

Tell the children to find a partner and to stand across from their partner (B_1 and L_1 are partners). Call out an -ing word—laughing. B_1 and L_1 should exchange places one at a time. As B_1 moves he should express "laughing" in a big manner, with both sounds and large movements (e.g., a boisterous laugh with accompanying movements). As the first person moves from the "Little" group, tell her to show "laughing" in a little way, both verbally and nonverbally (possibly a little "tee-hee" on tiptoe). Continue with these "exchanges," giving each pair of partners a different -ing word, until the entire "Big" group is on the "Little" side, and vice versa. Start again with a new set of -ing words, having former "Big" group members now do "little" expressions and former "Little" group members do "big" expressions. Encourage the children to make full use of both verbal and nonverbal expressions of words.

MOTIVATIONAL HINTS/SPECIAL CONSIDERATIONS: Preface the activity with a brief discussion of big and little sounds, gestures, movements. You might say, for example, "Did you ever see a person sneezing in a big way? How might that sound? What would he or she do with his or her body?"

If a child doesn't wish to move across the room "in front of everybody," let him express his -ing word in place. Hopefully he'll see that all responses are acceptable, so no one wins or loses. His partner may do the activity in his place, also.

VARIATIONS: For younger children you may want to give an -ing word to the entire "Big" group first and have them all move across the room together, and then give the same -ing word to the "Little" group, having them move into the "Big" group's space. After the whole group feels comfortable, you may decide to use the activity as described above.

F. MIRRORS

OBJECTIVE: To practice concentrating and moving while following someone's lead; to encourage cooperation.

DESCRIPTION: Have the children find a partner and partner spaces. Begin with partners sitting on the floor facing each other. Explain that one of the partners is the person, the other the mirror. The mirror must do exactly the same movements as the person "looking into the mirror." If the person raises an arm and tilts his head, the mirror must do the same movement. Tell the mirror that he must remember he is a mirror, that is, if the person uses his left arm, the mirror must use her right arm. Coach the person to move slowly and carefully so that the mirror can follow exactly. You may want to try giving specific suggestions first, such as "brush your hair" or "wash your hands"; then let the person move on his or her own. When you feel that the mirror can follow the person's movements exactly, have the partners stand up and use their whole bodies. Coach the mirror to concentrate on facial expressions as well as on physical movements. After a while, have the partners change roles and repeat the activity.

MOTIVATIONAL HINTS/SPECIAL CONSIDERATIONS: Occasionally you may have children who feel that they must outwit (compete with) their mirror. Remind them that cooperation is the primary purpose—not seeing how fast they can move. You may tell them that you want to see if you can tell who the mirror is and who the person is. If you can easily tell which is which, then the partners have not been concentrating.

After the class understands the basic movements, stimulate their imaginations by giving specific directions of increasing difficulty. For example: brush your hair, get dressed, make faces in the mirror, do a dance step, wash the mirror. Remind them that mirror images shouldn't touch the person; they may be as close as possible without touching.

VARIATIONS: "Opposites" is a challenging variation and should be used only after the children are fairly proficient with the basics of the game.

"Opposites" is played by the mirror moving in the opposite direction from the person. For example, the person raises his right foot forward—the mirror must put his left foot back. If the person stretches, the mirror should crouch, and so on. Specific movements are more challenging. Brushing the person's hair forward may result in brushing the mirror's hair back. Hopping up and down could become hopping down and up—syncopated. If the person swings her arms from right to left, the mirror would then swing his arms from his right to left (remember, the mirror is facing the person).

Two or more opposite movements are even more challenging. If the person pats his head and rubs his stomach while jumping up and down, would the mirror rub his head and pat his stomach while jumping down and up? Have fun with these; the children will.

G. SHADOWING

OBJECTIVE: To encourage cooperation, provide self-control and concentrate on physical movement.

DESCRIPTION: You may want to use this activity in conjunction with "Mirrors" (see page 47).

Take the children outside on a sunny day. Place them in a straight line so their shadows are in front of them. Then ask them to make straight lines with parts of their bodies; they can raise their right legs, right arms and so on. Then have them make curved lines by rounding their arms, hanging forward, etc. Encourage them to see what their shadows can and cannot do (shadows cannot imitate facial expressions).

Ask the kids to go back inside the classroom and find a partner. One will be the person, the other the shadow. This time, have the shadow stand next to the person rather than in front (as in "Mirrors"). Then, have the person do an action and the shadow follow. The goal is to have the shadow perform the action at the same time as the person. Coach the person to act out a variety of feelings (happy, scared) with her body so the shadow can follow.

H. PUPPET ON A STRING

OBJECTIVE: To promote mimetic stretching and other exercises.

DESCRIPTION: This activity is really a spinoff of "Being Things" (see page 29) but is an excellent imaginative warm-up exercise. You will need a puppet for demonstration purposes; a string puppet is best, but a hand puppet works fine.

Have the children find their own spaces. Then stand in front of them and have them observe the way a puppet moves. While you work the puppet, ask, "Does a puppet move just like a person or are there differences? What are the differences?" Have the children stay in their own spaces and move just the way you move your puppet.

Tell them they must watch your puppet carefully. A good way to begin is with the puppet totally inanimate on the floor. Have the kids imagine how it feels for a puppet master to slowly bring a puppet to life. Wiggle the puppet's arm up and down. Shake the puppet's head. Have the puppet stand up (his legs are wobbly). Remind the children to feel like a puppet and to focus their attention on what the real puppet is doing. From here it is up to you. You can have the "puppets" do exercises (touch toes, stretch, kick, etc.); move fast or slowly in their own spaces; work on left-right discrimination (turn the puppet's back to the class); or any number of movements or games.

MOTIVATIONAL HINTS: If you feel that you are losing attention, let the puppet be limp (inanimate) on the floor or desk. Then begin again slowly.

VARIATIONS: Once most of the group are skilled at attention focus and mimetics in their own spaces, there are several variations that you might want to try:

1. Older children, after they've worked mimetically, can pair up, with one person being the puppet master and the other the puppet. Remind them that they should cooperate, working slowly at first, and that the puppet should really feel only the "strings" that the puppet master is pulling. Have them work in a confined space and, after a while, have them switch roles.

2. After working in confined spaces and developing the feeling of moving like a puppet, ask each child to imagine that he has a giant puppet master of his own. Let him explore the general space, moving like a puppet. You can call quick stops and starts and use music.

I. INANIMATE OBJECTS

OBJECTIVE: To use imagination and the body to give movement and feelings to inanimate (imaginary) objects.

DESCRIPTION: This activity can be used in conjunction with "Being Things" (see page 29).

Have the children find their own spaces. As a preliminary activity, name any specific object (a vacuum cleaner, a ball, snow, etc.) and have the children become that object, moving when you say "GO." Tell them to remain in their own spaces and stop moving when you say "FREEZE." After a few objects have been acted out, ask the children to find a partner. One partner will be the object, the other will use the object in any way he or she chooses. Call out an object—a tractor, a banana, a pillow, or whatever—and the object-child must allow her partner to "use" her (gently, of course), i.e., turn on the tractor, peel the banana, fluff up the pillow. On "CHANGE," the object becomes the object user and vice versa.

You may want to use this activity to reinforce the concepts of categories and groups and freedom of choice. Call out a category (machines, toys, hardware, school supplies, kitchen gadgets, appliances, etc.). Then have each set of partners decide which object within the given category they would like to "bring to life." When all sets are ready, say "GO" and have the partners move. After a short period of time, "freeze" the group. Ask every set of partners what object they had in mind, saying, "What did you use?" "Did you have a job to do with your object?" Or you may wish to have those partners who choose to demonstrate their object to the class and have a guessing game.

MOTIVATIONAL HINTS/SPECIAL CONSIDERATIONS: You may want to brainstorm categories and objects with your children, writing them on the board before you start the activity. The kids can then use the list as stimuli. Ask the group which category they would like to choose their objects from. As the group is doing the activity, wander around and give positive reinforcement.

When using categories, make sure that each set of partners has a specific object in mind before you start the activity. For those who need help in choosing, ask pertinent questions like, "What are appliances?" "What do they do?" "How do they move?" Help the kids envision their object by saying, "Is your object large or small, loud or silent?" "Does it have a motor?" "Can you fit it in your hand?" "Do you always have to use the whole object or just part of it (e.g., the hose of a cannister vacuum cleaner or an entire upright vacuum)?" Explain that the whole body doesn't always have to be used—the "object" may use just his or her foot and leg as a hammer, for example—and the partner doesn't have to try to lift his partner's whole body.

VARIATIONS: Here are two more activities:

1. For more advanced imagination practice, try giving other qualities to the objects. Call out the object (say, a firecracker), and add a few descriptive words: an old, tired firecracker that has lost some of its spark; a spanking new firecracker; a small firecracker; an angry firecracker. When using categories, add the new dimensions, but generalize (e.g., school supplies that have been left out in the rain for ten years). Add the dimensions after the children have chosen their objects; call out the characteristics as the objects are moving to keep spontaneity in the activity.

2. To expand this activity, create a problem that the partners must

solve using an object. For example, you want to give a toy to your younger brother—which toy do you think he'd like? Use the toy to make sure it works.

J. PARTNER STATUES

OBJECTIVE: To practice sustaining a position for a length of time; to practice cooperating in pairs; to learn to work out imaginative challenges physically and verbally.

DESCRIPTION: Have the children find partners and get in their own spaces. Tell one child of each pair that she will be the statue, the other the statue maker. Then tell the children that you will give them a word—a general word, such as machine, vegetable, animal, or a specific word, such as happy, ball, banana. As you give the word, say, happy, have the maker hold one or both hands of the statue and swing it around in a small circle. Then, tell the statue maker to let go of the statue and sit down on the floor. Have the statue hold the position in which it ends up. Ask each statue (still in position) what it is and why its position is "happy." Then have the partners change roles and repeat the activity with another word.

MOTIVATIONAL HINTS/SPECIAL CONSIDERATIONS: Coach the children to use their whole body and employ facial expressions. Also, be certain that the statue makers use control when swinging their partners; the purpose of the swing is to give momentum to the statue, not to have it fall and get hurt.

VARIATIONS: Here are a few similar activities:

1. Still in partners, have the statue and the statue maker facing each other. Tell the maker she must use only one finger to "mold" the statue. For example, on your directive (happy), the maker may use one finger to move the statue's head to one side, raise the statue's wrist, lift the statue's leg. Wherever the maker stops the statue's body, that's where the statue must remain. Coach the statue to remain loose and to concentrate just on that part of her body directed by the maker's finger. Coach the maker to move slowly and carefully. Repeat the activity using different words and having partners change roles.

2. This variation is done individually, by half the class at a time. You may wish to use a drum or clap your hands for a beat.

Encourage the students to react with their bodies to each beat of the drum (clap)—stretching high, crouching low, swinging to left, right. At one point as they move, say "FREEZE. You now have become statues. You are frozen in the middle of some action. Try to think what action you were doing before you froze. Were you throw-

ing something? Catching something?" Have half the class stay frozen while the other half tries to guess what action the statues were doing. Encourage a variety of suggestions—remember, there may not be one "right" answer. Ask more specific questions, such as, "When you were picking something up, was it heavy, light? Small, large?" Challenge the kids' imagination. Repeat the activity and have the statues become guessers.

3. Have half the class form a group statue around a theme, while the other half observes, then guesses the theme. Or, have half the class make a collective machine or musical group (with some kids being musicians and some being instruments) with each individual contributing an appropriate sound or motion.

Chapter

3

Activities That Teach And Reinforce Academic Skills

he activities in this chapter are designed to teach and reinforce academic skills and concepts through the use of the body and imagination. For more ideas in this area, see the Resource section at the back of this book.

A. GEOMETRIC CRAWLING SHAPES

This activity, "Giant Cardboard Letters" (page 57) and "Bodies as Letters/Numbers"(page 63) are the only activities in this book which require equipment that you are not likely to have on hand, namely large plywood or cardboard shapes and letters. The time spent making these shapes and letters, however, will be well worth it, since they will enable you to encompass cognitive, affective and psychomotor aspects of learning in one activity.

EQUIPMENT: A variety of large and small colored shapes (see "How to Make Shapes" on page 90).

OBJECTIVE: To reinforce the following concepts through movement: following directions; colors; small-large; inside-outside; around-through; over-under; triangles-squares-circles-rectangles; tracing; balancing; on-off; left-right; body parts; above-below; perimeter-area; concentric.

DESCRIPTION: Depending on class size, you may want to split your class into two groups so that each child will have a shape.

Have the children find their own spaces and sit down. Then put the shapes you have made on the floor in a line. Call a child's name and say, for example, "Hop to the small red triangle, pick it up and walk back to your space." Continue with each child, varying the locomotor movement, until all the children have a shape and have returned to their places. Then you can give movement challenges like these:

CONCEPT	CHALLENGE
Size	• All those with large shapes, stand up.
	• All those with small shapes, jump in place.
Color	• All those with large red shapes, hop on your left foot (vary movement).
	• All those with small blue shapes, take one step to the right (vary color and size).
Shape	• All those with large yellow triangles, skip to the wall (vary shape).
Around	• Everyone put your shape down. Hop around your shape.
Through	• Put your head through your shape (vary body part).
In-out	• Move inside your shape. Put your hands inside your shape. Put your foot in and then take it out of your shape. Leave your head out of your shape, but put the rest of your body in your shape. Hold the shape in front of you and pretend you are inside a TV looking out.
Over-under	• Move over your shape. How many different ways can you do this?
Balancing	• Walk on your shape. Balance yourself. Make sure you stay on your shape (perimeter can be introduced or reinforced here).
Left-right	• Place your right arm in your shape. Now your left foot. Put your left arm and right foot in your shape (vary combinations of body parts).
Above-below	• Be below your shape. Be above your shape.
Sequence	• Hop outside, then jump inside your shape. (Give all directions before having the children move; vary the combinations of directions.) Run around the circle, go through the square (you can set up an obstacle course with the shapes).
Tracing	• Trace your shape with your hand, foot, etc. (You may even wish to have the children trace their shapes on to large pieces of paper, cut them out, color them and make a "Shape Chain" for the classroom.)
Concentric	• Put a small shape inside a large shape.

MOTIVATIONAL HINTS/SPECIAL CONSIDERATIONS: After you have used the shapes to reinforce learning concepts, you may wish to expand the children's creativity and imagination by "changing" the shapes into something else. For example, you might say, "You're in your car, driving along (the children can sit in their shapes and "drive" them), when your car becomes a frog pond . . . what would you be then?" Make your stories simple, changing the shapes and allowing children to use them as imaginary objects.

VARIATIONS: You can use the shapes for a beginning lesson in geometry by having the children measure the length, width, area, perimeter, circumference, etc., of their shape. Supply each child with a ruler or meter stick.

B. GIANT CARDBOARD LETTERS

EQUIPMENT: A variety of colored letters, at least one per child (see "How To Make Shapes" on page 90).

OBJECTIVE: To reinforce various learning concepts through movement.

DESCRIPTION: Before beginning this activity, review all the things you can do with shapes (see "Geometric Crawling Shapes" on page 57). You can do most of them with letters, too. Here are other activities you can do.

To begin, place the letters you have made on the floor in random order. Ask a few children to put the letters in alphabetical order. When they're in order, have each child choose his or her favorite letter (or second favorite in case of duplicates) and find his or her own space. Then adapt the same learning concepts and challenges used in "Geometric Crawling Shapes." You can add two other concepts—straight-curved and vowels—to the list.

Here's another activity: Once the children have chosen their favorite letter, ask all of them at your signal to be something that begins with that letter. Ask, "Does your something move? What does it do? Show me." You may have to help those with Q's, X's or other difficult letters. "Can your something move quickly . . . slowly . . . up and down? Make your something have feelings—let it be happy, sad, angry." Have the children act out their "something" one at a time and let the other kids guess what it is.

A number of games can begin with children standing in a straight line, holding their letters in alphabetical order. After designating a line several feet or yards from them, have the kids move to the line in any of the following ways:

1. Colors—"All blue letters (red letters, etc.) run to the line."

59

2. Shapes—"All *round* letters (C, G, O, Q) skip to the line . . . all letters with *straight* lines (N, M, T) skip to the line . . . all straight and curved letters (R, P, B, D) skip to the line . . . all letters with *up and down* lines (I, H, L) skip to the line." Continue in this way as you wish. Watch to make sure that only those children with letters having the characteristics you call out move to the line and use the movement you designate.

3. Vowels-consonants—"All *vowels* run to the line. All *consonants* slide on their feet to the line."

4. Alphabetical order—"All letters that come *before* M run to the line . . . all letters between P and Z hop to the line . . . all letters *after* M jump to the line." For more fun—"All letters between A and Z run to the line!"

5. Sounds of letters—"All letters with sounds made by putting your lips together jump to the line . . . all letters with sounds made by keeping your mouth open (lips apart) skip to the line." Or, for a more individual activity, "the sounds 'Buh-A-T' run to the line . . . the sound of 'S-S-S' skip to the line (two letters—C and S)." You may want to make a list of words to say phonetically so that you use all the letters you have (see "Motivational Hints/Special Considerations" for more on this). CVC (consonant-vowel-consonant) words are excellent for beginners.

6. Word scramble—Have a prepared list of words to be unscrambled. Then say, for example, "The letters P, N and A run to the line. Try to unscramble yourselves to make a word. Class, can you help them?" (PAN) "Can you make another word using the same letters but putting them in a different order?" Have P, N and A skip back to their places. Call out other letters to be unscrambled, increasing the difficulty of the words depending upon the ability of your class (or specific child, if you want only one child to unscramble the letters).

You can also start activities by placing the letters randomly around the room. You'll need 3″ × 5″ cards with lower-case letters (one to a card) and a record player or tambourine (hand claps or whistling will also work). Tell the class to skip around the room, making sure that no one steps on any of the letters. Then say, "When the music stops (or I stop clapping), touch the capital letter on the floor that is the same letter as this one" (hold up a card with a lower-case letter on it). If your group is too large for everyone to touch only one letter, have several letters printed on each card. Then the children can touch the letter each is nearest to when the music stops.

For a more advanced activity, have the children touch the letters with specific body parts (left hand, right foot). Vary the body parts and letters.

MOTIVATIONAL HINTS/SPECIAL CONSIDERATIONS: To re-motivate the children, have them trade letters. Let them find their own spaces, then trade with the child next to them and sit down. Use a signal ("CHANGE") to control the changes.

You may also remind the children to think about their letters and to pay attention. Make this a game rather than an order: "Pretend you are this letter; think to yourself what sound you make, what you look like, what color you are."

If you have more than 26 children, ask them to double up on some letters so that two children have/are one letter (try having them hold the letter between them). This may take lots of cooperation from the kids since one may move faster than the other.

If you have less than 26 children, have some children become two letters, but make sure that neither letter is one which is used very often.

C. BODIES AS LETTERS/NUMBERS

(This activity may be used after or before "Giant Cardboard Letters.")
OBJECTIVE: To promote body flexibility and imagination.
DESCRIPTION: When the children are standing in alphabetical order with their letters, have them place their letters on the floor behind them. Tell them, "I am going to change your body into your letter. Think silently how you will look—curved, straight up and down, diagonal, round. When I wave my magic spoon (or any other device you wish) and sing my song (you can make up your own), in slow motion, start changing your body into your letter. By the time I finish my song you will have become your letter. Freeze as that letter."

Begin to wave your arm slowly and sing a song, for example:
"When I wave my magic spoon, a letter you will be.
Very very soon, people letters I will see. FREEZE."

Walk down the line and say the alphabet, acknowledging the letters you see.

You may repeat the activities used in "Giant Cardboard Letters," or you may wish to try these:

1. Have the A through L's sit down facing the rest of the letters, who are standing. Have the standing letters scramble themselves, resume their letter shape and freeze at your command. Ask those sitting to guess what letters those standing are. Repeat with the A through L's scrambling and freezing.

2. Break your class into groups of two, three or four, depending upon the size of the group and/or the letters you wish to reinforce.

You may verbally give each group a letter or have the group choose its own letter. (Stress that it is all right for two groups to have the same letter.) Have each group form its letter together. For example, a group of four may want to become the letter W, or you may have them become an E. You can have all groups "freeze" at once and you guess the letters, or one group at a time "freeze" while the other groups guess the letter.

3. Have the children guess each other's letters or have teams make words that other teams guess. Some letters are harder to make than others, but ask the children to explain their letter if no one guesses it.

MOTIVATIONAL HINTS/SPECIAL CONSIDERATIONS: When the children each become their own letter, watch for reversibility. The letter should be correct when it is facing you or, if it's on the floor, when you are looking down on it.

Do not expect perfection. Some letters just won't look like the letters they should be, partially because of inflexible bodies. Encourage the kids to use all parts of their body. For example, an L made with an arm sticking out will not look like an L. Ask the child if he or she can think of any other way an L could be made. (Some letters are more easily made lying down than standing up.) Remember, though, that the attempt is more important than the final product. The process of motivation and the message that letters and words are fun are most important.

VARIATIONS: Here are a few other ways to encourage body flexibility and imagination:

1. Do these same activities with numbers: individually, in groups of two (tens place), three (hundreds place), etc.

2. Try adding one child (number) to another to get a sum (a third child-number).

3. A more advanced activity would be to have groups of three, four or five and lists of three-, four- or five-letter words. Each group would choose a word (perhaps out of a hat); then each child would form his or her body into one of the letters and have the rest of the class guess the word. You might try sentences after that.

D. MOVING TO SOUNDS IN A CIRCLE

OBJECTIVE: To practice auditory discrimination using physical movement.

DESCRIPTION: Form a circle with the children. Tell them to listen for a certain sound (for example, "Buh" for "B"). Say, "When you hear that sound, sit down. Until you hear that sound, everyone hold hands and walk to the left." As you are walking, repeat different letter sounds (K-K-K, S-S-S, etc.). After a short time, say a word that contains a "B" sound. The children should all sit down. **MOTIVATIONAL HINTS/SPECIAL CONSIDERATIONS:** Be sure that you do not sit down first; let the children figure it out. If no child sits down, you may want to use a visual stimulus. Put a letter drawn on construction paper (or use a letter from "Giant Cardboard Letters") in the center of the circle and have the children walk around it. For younger children, keep the physical movement the same for the entire activity (see Variation 1 below for older children). Do not try to teach more than one concept per activity period, unless you think the children can handle it.

VARIATIONS: These variations will be progressively more challenging:

1. Change the physical movement after you have played the game a few times. For example: "When you hear the sound, touch your knees . . . touch your toes . . . put your hands on your head . . . kick your foot into the circle . . . squat . . . go down on all fours." Use the movements one at a time, or two in succession if the children can handle it.

2. Change the sound you use. Try animal sounds (the physical movement can coincide with the sound, e.g., "When you hear the sound of a horse, become a horse"). You can try machine sounds, sounds in nature or a variety of others. You may wish to prepare a list of sounds in different categories so that you can keep the sounds going as the children move around.

3. You may also try this activity with children in their own spaces, walking around the room at random. You can change the sound and the movement as they walk.

E. BEING THINGS WITH PHONICS

OBJECTIVE: To reinforce beginning word sounds with physical movement.

DESCRIPTION: Ask the children to get in their own spaces. Explain that you will say a word and each child is to think of something that begins with that same beginning sound. Use "FREEZE" and "MOVE" whenever you want the children to "freeze" as that word or to move in his or her own space as that word. There are myriads of possibilities. For example, try the sound "Buh" (letter B). The children could choose action words, inanimate objects, animate objects, emotions, qualities (bend, box, bear, bored, bright). After you "freeze" them, guess or ask each child what word he or she is.

You can use any letter and, if you wish, keep the choice of pos-

sibilities narrow (a good idea for younger children). "Choose a word that begins with the sound that is an animal (turtle for 'tuh') . . . that doesn't move . . . that is something you can touch."

MOTIVATIONAL HINTS/SPECIAL CONSIDERATIONS: If a child cannot think of a word, tell him to look around the room and find an object that begins with that letter. If you notice that a child does not move when you say "MOVE," remember that she may have chosen something that doesn't move (a blackboard, for example).

VARIATIONS: Here are three other ways to use this activity:

1. Use words that begin with consonant blends.
2. Use words that rhyme (this is much more advanced).
3. Use cardboard letters as visual stimuli. Have a child hold a letter so everyone can see or put it on the blackboard.

F. BODY PARTS UP AND DOWN

OBJECTIVE: To reinforce basic number concepts through individual movement.

DESCRIPTION: This idea has been around for quite a while. It's simple, kids love it and it has a lot of variation. You'll need several 5" ×8" cards with one number printed on each, or blackboard space to write the numbers on.

Have the children randomly space themselves within sight and sound of you. Tell them that when you say "GO" and for as long as the music continues they are to move in a specified manner. (For music you may hit a tambourine or a tom-tom, clap hands or play a record.)Give the kids specific motor tasks (spin, hop, run) and vary the amount of imagination involved in the task (move like a motorcycle, jump like a frog). (For more ideas, see "Being Things" in Chapter 2 and "Moving Through Space" in Chapter 1.)

Tell the children that as soon as the music stops they are to place the same number of body parts down on the ground as the number on the card that you hold up. That's all there is to it. Start simply and slowly, but urge the kids to respond quickly.

It is very likely that many of the children will simply stand on their two feet when they see the "2" card. Encourage them, though, to express the number individualistically. Ask them what two parts of their bodies are touching the ground. Probably they will say "My two feet." Reach down and strongly touch one child's feet while counting "1, 2." Now say, "Is there another way that you could have two parts touching the ground?" One child may put one hand and one foot down on the ground, another may do a handstand. Tell the children that in this game there are a lot of ways to get the right answer and that "their way" is important. "Let's do some more numbers now and see if we can see a lot of different ways to express them." Repeat the process, giving a movement task, then stopping the music and holding up a number. Pick out individuals again and use the touch-count method as described. Acknowledge unusual solutions.

MOTIVATIONAL HINTS/SPECIAL CONSIDERATIONS: Let's say you held up the number 9 and you noticed that Suzie is standing on one leg and has four fingers down on the ground. At first sight this looks incorrect but there's a simple way of checking the answer. Ask Suzie what the number is that you held up. If she doesn't know it, tell her. If she does know it, ask her what her nine parts are. She may well tell you that they are the five toes on her foot and four fingers, adding up to nine. Her position could have also indicated the number 5 (four fingers and one foot) but by asking her you can determine her knowledge of the concept. Be sure to touch and count the parts out loud.

There will be times when children will not have the right number of parts. You can correct their error by counting and touching the parts they do have down and pointing out that that's not the correct number. You might ask them if they could add or subtract a part or two to make the correct number. Then recount-touch the correct number of parts. You should keep the pace quick, however, and not spend too much time talking.

VARIATIONS: Once the children have gotten used to the idea of "number of parts down" you can have them put different parts "up" in the air when the music stops. You might also use dots or other objects instead of numbers, and try beginning addition and subtraction problems on the cards, having the kids tell the answers with their bodies.

$5 - 3 =$ (2 body parts $8 + 1 =$ (9 body parts, on the floor)   etc.)

Another variation would be for the class to form seated groups of different sizes, depending on the number that you held up.

G. GIANT CHALK LETTERS AND NUMBERS

OBJECTIVE: To reinforce basic number concepts through group organization and cooperation.

DESCRIPTION: This is another way to practice number, letter and sound recognition. To prepare you will need to write several large numbers, letters or letter blends in chalk in various places on an asphalt playground area (you may also wish to have flash cards on hand). Do this before the class comes outside. Make the numbers or letters large enough so that the entire class can stand comfortably on each letter or number and spread them out so that the kids will have to hunt for the correct response. Your layout might look something like the accompanying illustration.

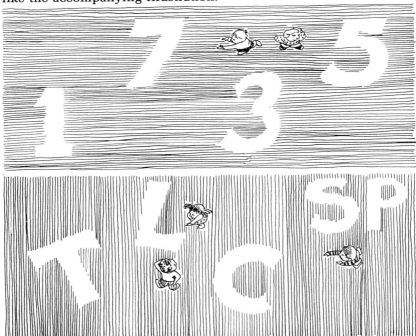

When the figures have been drawn, stand on one side of the area and have the group randomly spread out in front of you within hearing distance. Present your challenges to them visually (with flash cards), verbally or both visually and verbally. Here are some example challenges:

1. "When I say 'GO' I want everyone in the class to be on the giant number that is the answer to this problem (hold up a card that shows $4 + 3 = \_$) and to have *that* many body parts up in the air (see "Body Parts Up and Down" on page 67) or down on the ground. GO." The children should run to the giant 7 and should put seven body parts up in the air. The class collectively (from an aerial view) will be a giant 7 and individually will indicate the correct response to the problem. Again, emphasize quickness of response. Variations can be as simple or complex as you wish.

2. With letters or blends your challenges may again vary in com-

plexity. For example, you can say, "When I say 'GO,' everyone stand on the letter that 'lion' begins with and act like a lion." Or "When I say 'GO,' everyone stand on one of the letters that make the sound 'SP' and do something that begins with those letters." Another challenge might have the entire class stand on the "S" or the "P" and spin.Try to fool the group once in a while by giving them their next challenge in this manner: After everyone is standing on the "S" or "P," say, "Now run to one of the two letters that the word spaghetti begins with and pretend that you're eating spaghetti. GO!" Some children may run around but those that understand the blend quickly will stay where they are and begin acting out the challenge.

H. GRIDS AND MORE GRIDS

OBJECTIVE: To teach and reinforce the concepts of numbers, letters, beginning sounds and words, all in combination with expressive movement.

DESCRIPTION: This is a simple activity that requires about two minutes of preparation and has an infinite amount of variations. All you need is a lined circle or rectangle (your school playground may have one or you can line one out on an asphalt area) that is large enough to fit your whole class in, some chalk and your imagination.

First, divide your circle (rectangle) with chalk lines into a grid of approximately 9-12 spaces. In each of these spaces, print in chalk something that you would like to teach/reinforce. Then have all of the children randomly spread out inside the circle and move in the manner and direction that you wish them to. For example, when you say "GO" and for as long as you keep clapping (or hitting a drum or tambourine) they should *hop* in a counterclockwise direction, staying inside the circle and being careful not to crash into anyone. You may have them move in as simple or complex a manner as you wish (see "Moving Through Space"), combining imaginative elements (hopping like frogs; walking angrily) with basic movements.

When the clapping or music stops, the kids immediately stop in whatever box (grid) they are in and do what the grid tells them to do. Before the clapping or music starts, if you are working with numbers, say, "When the music stops put the same number of body parts on the ground as the number in your box." Or, for letters, "Be something that begins with the letter in your box." You can use numbers, letters, blends, beginning addition or subtraction problems or words.

MOTIVATIONAL HINTS/SPECIAL CONSIDERATIONS: After the children have responded to what is in their grid, check their answers. For example, say, "How many parts do you have down on the ground? What are they? All right, let's count them . . . very good. Are we all ready to go again? GO."

When dealing with math operations you will probably want to start with just one, for example, only addition problems in the grids. As skills advance you can mix up the possibilities any way that you like. The students would still indicate their answer by placing body parts on the ground or up in the air.

Try to keep the pace of this activity quick. Spot check, give the kids individual attention and verbally acknowledge creative solutions, for instance, a hand and foot on the ground as opposed to two feet for a person in the "2" box. Some children may respond better in this mode because the activity is very concrete and involves multiple senses (body emotions, intellect) but you can help everyone by "floating and teaching." For example, one of the kids in the "M" box might be a motorcycle, another might be a monster and a third might not recognize the letter. You could say to that child, "What is Susie doing?" (being a motorcycle) "Can you hear the sound of the letter at the beginning of the word motorcycle?" (mmmotorcycle) "What do you think that letter is now?" (M) "Right, very good."

Here are a few ways to use this format:

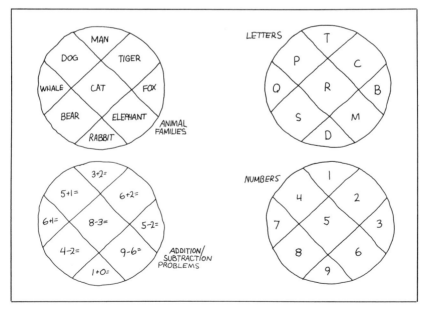

I. MOVEMENT WORD SIGNS AND VARIATIONS

OBJECTIVE: To provide imaginative movement challenges that teach and reinforce letter, sound and vocabulary concepts.

DESCRIPTION: Think of a number of words that describe things that move or movement qualities and write each of those words on a large piece of cardboard. Have the group randomly spread out in their own spaces. Then use your cardboard signs to provide movement challenges for the children to do either in their own space or in the general space. Explain to the group that you have signs that will tell them to move in different ways or like different things. Stand where you can be seen by all and tell the kids to watch you carefully since you will be making some quick changes with your signs.

Then begin. Hold up signs like HOP or JUMP or SPIN. Hold up signs like MOTORCYCLE or FROG or FLOWER. Hold up signs like SLOWLY or STRONG or SILLY. Keep the words as simple or complex as you like. Start with single signs changed quickly and gradually move to combinations of two signs: HOP QUICKLY or SILLY BEAR. Give the children encouragement and positive reinforcement and point out particularly good solutions to your challenges. Remind them to focus on what the words say. If things get a little too crazy, hold up SIT QUIETLY signs or a STOP sign.

Chapter

4

New Games *

ew Games aren't necessarily new—some have been played for a long time. What's "new" about New Games is the way they're played. New Games encourage creative play and emphasize the joy of participation. They also produce in the players high energy, self-exploration and social sharing. More than a list of activities, they are an attitude toward play, an attitude that people of all ages can and should play together for the fun of it; that laughter and physical and mental activity are wholesome; that people can create new games.

What follows is just a sampling of New Games. They are a natural extension of what we have been talking about throughout this book.

A. KNOTS

OBJECTIVE: To "untie" a chain of people through verbal and physical cooperation.

DESCRIPTION: This game can be played inside or out. Try it first with a few kids (perhaps 10 or 12), then enlarge the group if you like.

Have the children stand in a circle with you shoulder to shoulder and place your hands in the center, away from the children to either

*Special thanks to the New Games Foundation, P.O. Box 7901, San Francisco, California 94120 for permission to share much of the material in this chapter. The Foundation is a nonprofit organization created in 1974 to foster and communicate the concept of New Games. Dedicated to encouraging individual creative action, they perform a seed function helping individuals and groups to initiate their own New Games projects. To this end they have offered training programs and presentations on New Games in over 70 cities in 22 states and 4 foreign countries. They also cosponsor tournaments and are a resource for New Games equipment and materials.

side of you. Have everyone grab hands (you,too) but make sure that no one holds both hands with the same person or the hand of a child right next to them. You may direct the children to take the hand of two kids across from them.

Now untie the knot! The object is to end up with a circle or straight line of hand-holding children. There are two approaches: doing and talking. For the first, select a "doer," who should immediately begin crawling under, over, around and through the maze of linked hands, trying to untangle them. For the second method, choose a "talker," who should analyze the situation and direct others: "Sheila, you go under to your right first, then Marc!" However the knot becomes untied is fine as long as hands stay locked.

You can direct the group to tangle up in different ways: "John, you step over Mary's arm, Sally you crawl under Suzy's legs" and so on. Then see how long it takes the kids to get out. You can also try having opposing teams. Emphasize communication and use "Knot-aid," breaking a pair of hands and reconnecting at a better place if the task becomes too frustrating.

B. BLOB (also known as Boa Constrictor, an African folk game)

OBJECTIVE: To provide high energy in a cooperative/competitive tag game.

DESCRIPTION: Any number of children can play this game. First, set up boundaries (not too far apart) in the schoolyard. You may want to begin by being the "Blob." Chase the children within the marked area until you catch one. That child then grabs your hand and becomes part of the Blob. Now both you and your partner, still holding hands, catch others (only outside hands can capture) who also become part of the Blob. The Blob may either tag or encircle its prey. As the Blob grows, naturally, the runners dwindle.

One of the neat characteristics of the Blob is that it can split up into different numbers of smaller Blobs to snare runners; if the Blob is getting too long and/or cooperation is dwindling, you may want to subdivide it. The only stipulation to be made is that no one can split into an individual Blob; there must be at least two kids to a Blob.

When only one runner (or whatever number you choose) is left, you may want to have her begin again and become a new Blob. Encourage Blob huddles, Blob sounds and working together to develop strategies.

C. OHH-AHH (also called Zoom)

OBJECTIVE: To keep a combination sound-gesture going around in a circle; to promote concentration, high mental energy and increased attention span.

DESCRIPTION: Any number of children over 10 can play. Start with everyone standing (or seated) in a circle, holding hands. Give a quick squeeze to the hand of the child on your right. Have that child pass the squeeze along to the child on his right; before you know it, you'll have your original squeeze back again, in your left hand.

Keep passing the squeeze until it is traveling smoothly around the circle. Now speed up the action a bit and add sound. Squeeze and say "ohh," and have the children do the same. Next add "ahh," but send it in the opposite direction. Someone is going to get zapped between the "ohh" and the "ahh." The sounds can be sent with a deft exchange.

Now try reversing the flow. When someone gives you an "ohh," pass it back to him. When both "ohh" and "ahh" are traveling in the same direction, you can play tag, one trying to catch the other.

After the above games have been mastered, try transforming a sound-gesture by adding another action or changing a sound. Try it while sitting rather than standing, starting slowly and gradually increasing the speed and complexity. Try "zoom" in one direction and "beep" in the other.

D. SKIN THE SNAKE (also known as the Nerd Game)

OBJECTIVE: To provide a cooperative exercise and/or competition between two teams.

DESCRIPTION: This activity works best with 20 to 25 players per team (30 is O.K. too), so you may wish to ask another class to join you. Have the kids line up one behind the other and join them. Now reach between your legs with your left hand and grab the right hand of the child behind you. Have the child in front of you reach back to grab your right hand. When all hands are held, you're ready.

At a given signal, have the last person in line lie down on her back. The person in front of her should back up, straddle her body and lie down on his back right behind her, still holding hands. Continue until the whole team has moved backward over the growing line of prone bodies and slipped into place.

When the last person to lie down has touched his head to the ground, have him get up and start forward again, pulling everyone else up and along. In this manner the group will "Skin the Snake."

E. DUCKS AND COWS

OBJECTIVE: To have your class divide itself into two teams.

DESCRIPTION: Have everyone stand in a loosely constructed circle around you. Then whisper either the word "duck" or the word "cow" into each child's ear. The children are to close their eyes and, on your signal, make the sound of their given animal. As they say their sound they should keep their eyes closed and find and hold on to a person making the same sound.

When everyone is connected you'll have two groups, one of cows, the other of ducks, or you'll have a surge of humanity sounding like a barnyard.

VARIATIONS: This variation is known as "The Mating Game." You'll need several pairs of cards, enough for each child to receive one card. On each pair write the name of an animal.

Hand the cards out at random. On your signal have each child use sounds and gestures to act out the animal on his or her card. When two players realize they are being the same animal, they should stand together. Continue until everyone has found their mate.

F. PALM TREE/ELEPHANT/RACCOON

OBJECTIVE: To promote quick thinking and small-group cooperation within a large group.

DESCRIPTION: Have everyone in a circle with one person in the middle. Tell the children that they will be working together in groups of three to form either elephants, palm trees or raccoons. Illustrate the game by having the person in the center spin around and point to one child in the circle. That child will be the center of the construction (either palm tree, elephant or raccoon) and the child to his immediate left and immediate right will be the sides of the construction. Depending on what the center person calls out, the three children will act out one of the following things:

1. A palm tree. The center person should put her arms over her head, fingertips touching, to form the center leaf. The side people should do the same movement, tilting outward to form outer leaves.

2. An elephant. The center person should put his arms together, hanging in front of him, to form a trunk. Each side person should make a big semi-circle with his arms, touching one of the center person's ears to represent elephant ears.

3. A raccoon. The center person should place her cupped hands facing down in front of her mouth to mime a munching movement (like a rabbit eating a carrot). Each side person should place one hand, palm flat, over the center person's left or right eye. Collectively the three children are a raccoon.

Depending on who is pointed to, any person can be any role (side or center of any of the three constructions). Once the children have the idea, ask the child in the middle to spin around, point to a child and say "palm tree," "elephant" or "raccoon" and count quickly out loud to ten. During that time the child pointed to should assume the center position and the child to either side of her should assume the side position. If any of the threesome fails to act out their proper role within the time allotted, they must replace the person in the center of the circle. Encourage quickness and silliness; if you wish, you and the children can add new constructions to the choices.

G. THE KNEES GAME

OBJECTIVE: To promote group cooperation in solving a task; to end or begin a play-day with a feeling of unity.

DESCRIPTION: Have all the kids stand shoulder to shoulder in a big circle. Now have them turn to the right. Then have everybody sit down very gently on the knees of the person behind them in one of two ways. The slow and easy method is to have one child (select him ahead of time) lie on his back with his feet on the floor and his knees bent. The child in front of him should sit down on the first child's knees, forming a nice chair for the child in front of him to sit on, and on and on until the whole circle is seated. Emphasize gently sitting on each other's knees rather than laps. The crucial moment comes when the person on his back is hoisted up on the knees of the person behind him. Tell the kids to turn gradually at a slight angle as they sit down so they end up in a circle.

The fast and reckless method is for everyone to sit on their neighbor's knees at precisely the same moment. This is very impressive when it works and a spectacular flop when it doesn't. Once your group is comfortably seated, you might have everyone applaud themselves, wave or scratch their neighbor's back. Or try having them inch forward collectively. Falling apart is as much fun as getting together.

H. CATERPILLAR

OBJECTIVE: To teach group cooperation and encourage the idea that touch is O.K.

DESCRIPTION: Ask everyone to lie on their stomachs, side by side, all facing in one direction with hands above heads. Make sure the kids are really packed closely together and that there's lots of space around them. Then have the child at the end of the line roll over onto her neighbor and keep rolling down the row of bodies. After she's gotten over a few, ask the next child to start rolling, and so on. When

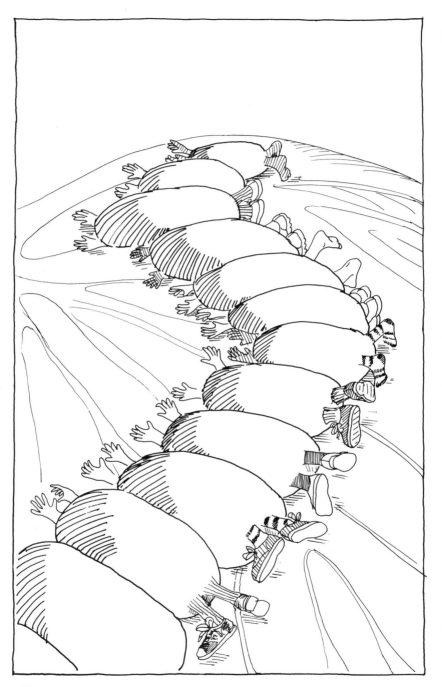

each roller gets to the end of the line she should lie on her stomach close to the last person in line. Emphasize that everyone should stay shoulder-to-shoulder close so there are no gaps. When lots of kids are in motion you'll think there's a human caterpillar in your room.

I. BALLOON BLOW-UP
OBJECTIVE: To promote group cooperation.
DESCRIPTION: This game is for the class balloon-blowing record. You'll need a number of balloons and a tolerance for popping. Give out several balloons each to half the group. They are to blow up the balloons, tie them and let them go while the other half of the class keeps them up in the air. When a balloon hits the floor, you should pop it or eliminate it from play. The goal is to fill the room with balloons being kept up in the air.
VARIATIONS: Have the kids hop on one foot or skip while trying to keep the balloons in the air. You can also put strings across the room and play "Balloon Volleyball."
SPECIAL CONSIDERATIONS: Some players may try to keep a balloon in the game after it has touched the floor. You may need several children to act as referees and to remove balloons that go out of play.

J. TWO HEADS ARE BETTER THAN ONE
OBJECTIVE: To teach partner cooperation.
DESCRIPTION: Have the group choose partners and form relay teams with not more than five pairs on each team. Give each team two "hats," made of paper bags stapled together at the bottom. At a signal, each pair must put on their "hats," run to a preselected goal line, turn around, run back to the starting line and pass the hats to the next pair. The hats must be kept on the runners' heads at all times; younger players may need to use their hands to hold their hats in place. The team that finishes first, having kept their hats on their heads, wins.
VARIATIONS: You can use other devices besides "hats" in this partner relay. Try having the pairs run with balls, balloons, beanbags or the like. You can ask them to jointly hold the object with various parts of their bodies.
SPECIAL CONSIDERATIONS: "Hats" may be torn apart during the races, so be sure to have extras on hand.

Epilogue

In this handbook are a number of specific creative play activities you can do with your class. But these games can be just the start of fun and learning through imaginative movement. Here are a number of ways you can expand or extend creative play with your children.

1. *Continue to involve yourself, your kids and their parents in creative play.* Expose yourself and your class to imaginative, creative events and activities. Attend, or better yet, organize a "Creative Play-day" at your school. Educate your children's parents about the ideas behind imaginative movement and New Games.

2. *Look for the possibilities of movement experiences all around you.* There are several suggestions for this in Chapter 1—play around with them.

3. *Put together a creative play space.* Better yet, let your children do it, or do it with them. Adventure playgrounds provide a marvelous opportunity for non-adult-centered play experiences.

4. *Invent your own imaginative movement game, or help your kids to create one.* The basic elements of a game are: a goal, rules, boundaries, opposition/sides, strategies, equipment, roles/ interaction patterns.

As an example, you can take an old favorite like baseball and change just one element, let's say equipment. Try playing baseball with a frisbee. Have the batter throw the frisbee and have the kids in the field try to catch it, throw the person out, etc. If you bring in a bunch of miscellaneous objects—old tires, dice, frisbees, Ping-Pong balls or whatever—a number of new games may be invented. And if you and your kids avoid too many rules and just experiment, the results will be enjoyable creative play.

Resources

American Adventure Play Association. Box 5430, Huntington Beach, Ca. 92646.

Anderson, Margaret et al. *Play with a Purpose: Elementary School Physical Education.* New York: Harper & Row, 1972.

Bower, Eli. *Learning to Play: Playing to Learn.* New York: Behavioral Publications, 1975.

Bower, Eli. "Play's the Thing," in *Games in Education and Development.* Springfield, Il.: C.C. Thomas, 1974.

Bruner, Jerome. "Play is Serious Business." *Psychology Today* (January 1975).

Caplan, Frank and Teresa. "Creativity Through Play," in *The Power of Play.* New York: Anchor Press/Doubleday, 1973.

Cratty, Bryant. *Active Learning: Games to Enhance Academic Abilities.* Englewood Cliffs, N.J.: Prentice-Hall, 1971.

Dauer, Victor. *Dynamic Physical Education for Elementary School Children.* Minneapolis: Burgess Publishing, 1975.

Dauer, Victor. *Essential Movement Experiences for Pre-School and Primary Children.* Minneapolis: Burgess Publishing, 1972.

De Mille, Richard. *Put Your Mother on the Ceiling: Children's Imagination Games.* New York: Viking Press, 1973.

Eberle, Robert. *Scamper: Games for Imagination Development.* Buffalo: D.O.K. Publishers Inc., 1971.

Fait, H. *Experiences in Movement: Physical Education for the Elementary School Child.* Philadelphia: Saunders, 1976.

Fandek, Ruth. *Classroom Capers: An Exploratory Approach to Movement Education in the Classroom.* Bellingham, Wa.: Education Designs, 1971.

Feitelson, D. and Ross, G. "The Neglected Factor—Play." *Human Development* (Volume 16, 1973).

Fluegelman, Andrew, ed. *The New Games Book.* Garden City, N.Y.: Doubleday/Dolphin, 1976. (New Games Foundation, P.O. Box 7901, San Francisco, Ca. 94120.)

Furlong, W. "The Flow Experience—The Fun in Fun." *Psychology Today* (June 1976).

Gilliom, B. *Basic Movement Education for Children: Rationale & Teaching Units.* Reading, Mass.: Addison-Wesley, 1970.

Gordon, William J. *Making It Strange.* New York: Harper & Row, 1968.

Halsey, E. and Porter, L. *Physical Education for Children.* New York: Holt, Rinehart and Winston, 1963.

Hart, Lenny. *Kids and Teachers: Partners in Excitement, Music in Motion Book 6.* San Rafael, Ca.: Education in Motion, 1974.

Hart, Lenny. *Sound and Action with Theory, Music in Motion Book 2.* San Rafael, Ca.: Education in Motion, 1974.

Hawes, Bess Lomax. "Law and Order on the Playground," in *Games in Education and Development*. Springfield, Il.: C.C. Thomas, 1974.

Hendricks, G. and Wells, R. *The Centering Book: Awareness Activities for Children, Parents and Teachers*. Englewood Cliffs, N.J.: Prentice-Hall, 1975.

Humphrey, J. and Sullivan, D. *Teaching Slow Learners Through Active Games*. Springfield, Il.: C.C. Thomas, 1973.

Jones, B. and Hawes, B. *Step It Down: Games, Plays, Songs and Stories from the Afro-American Heritage*. New York: Harper & Row, 1972.

Jones, Robert E. *Dramatic Imagination*. New York: Theatre Arts Books.

Leonard, George. "Winning Isn't Everything. It's Nothing." *Intellectual Digest* (October 1973).

Lewis, Howard and Streitfield, H. *Growth Games*. New York: Bantam, 1972.

Mc Caslin, Nellie. *Creative Dramatics in the Classroom*. New York: David McKay Co., 1974.

Michaelis, D. "Dramatic Emphasis" in "Dialog." *Teacher* (March 1976).

Michaelis, W. "Have You Ever Thought That . . . ?" *California Parks and Recreation Society Magazine*[CPRS] (August 1975).

Moffitt, Mary. "Play as a Medium for Learning." *Leisure Today*. American Alliance for Health, Physical Education, and Recreation [AAHPER] (June 1972).

Morris, G. *How to Change the Games Children Play*. Minneapolis: Burgess Publishing, 1976.

Mossten, M. *Developmental Movement*. Chicago: Merrill, 1965.

Mossten, M. *Teaching from Command to Discovery*. Belmont, Ca.: Wadsworth Publishing, 1972.

Mossten M. *Teaching Physical Education.* Chicago: Merrill, 1966.

Naake, Joan. "In New Games, No One's a Loser." *California Parks and Recreation Society Magazine* [CPRS] (April 1975).

Nobleman, Roberta. *Using Creative Dramatics Outside the Classroom.* New Plays for Children, P.O. Box 273, Rowaytown, Ct. 06853 (1974).

Orlick, Terry and Botterill, C. *Every Kid Can Win.* Chicago: Nelson-Hall, 1975.

Redl, F. "The Dimension of Games," in Avedon, E. and Sutton-Smith, B., *The Study of Games.* New York: Wiley, 1971.

Singer, Jerome. "Fantasy: the Foundation of Serenity." *Psychology Today* (July 1976).

Spolin, V. *Improvisation for the Theater: A Handbook of Teaching and Directing Techniques.* Evanston, Il.: Northwestern University Press, 1963.

Sutton-Smith, B. "Current Research and Theory on Play Games and Sport." Presentation to AMA Conference on Mental Health, Atlantic City, N.J. (July 3, 1975).

Sutton-Smith, B. "The Useless Made Useful: Play as Variability Training." *School Review* (February 1975).

Van Tassel, K. *Creative Dramatization.* New York: Macmillan, 1973.

How To Make Shapes and Letters

Giant shapes and capital letters can be made from either wood or cardboard. Plywood shapes are preferable, since they will be sturdier and last longer, but if a jigsaw is not available, cardboard will be easy to work with and less expensive to buy.

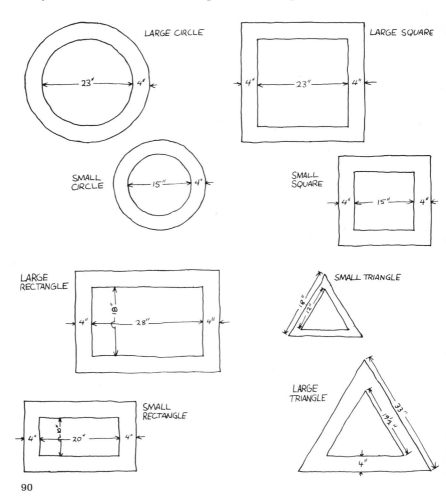

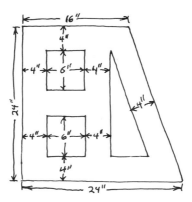

ABCDE
FGHIJ
KLMNO
PQRS
TUVW
XYZ

Notes

Notes